A MARGINAL SEA

Zoë Skoulding is Professor of Poetry and Creative Writing at Bangor University. Her collections of poetry (published by Seren Books) include *The Mirror Trade* (2004); *Remains of a Future City* (2008), shortlisted for Wales Book of the Year; *The Museum of Disappearing Sounds* (2013), shortlisted for Ted Hughes Award for New Work in Poetry; and *Footnotes to Water* (2019), which was a Poetry Book Society Recommendation and won the Wales Book of the Year Poetry Award 2020. In 2020 she also published *The Celestial Set-Up* (Oystercatcher) and *A Revolutionary Calendar* (Shearsman). Her critical work includes two monographs, *Contemporary Women's Poetry and Urban Space: Experimental Cities* (Palgrave Macmillan, 2013), and *Poetry & Listening: The Noise of Lyric* (Liverpool University Press, 2020). She received the Cholmondeley Award from the Society of Authors in 2018 for her body of work in poetry, and is a Fellow of the Learned Society of Wales.

A Marginal Sea

ZOË SKOULDING

CARCANET POETRY

First published in Great Britain in 2022 by
Carcanet
Alliance House, 30 Cross Street
Manchester, M2 7AQ
www.carcanet.co.uk

A CIP catalogue record for this book is
available from the British Library.

ISBN 978 1 80017 251 7

Book design by Andrew Latimer

The publisher acknowledges financial
assistance from Arts Council England.

Contents

A MARGINAL SEA

WEATHER THIS

Hello day, I wanted to talk to you about the weather,
though I never stop talking about it in blood and breath,
neck muscles, the way my feet slide across the pavement
or my head drinks up the light. But I only get so far

and then the horizon's wandered off again. This body's
opening to the pinkish gleam that rises – rose – on the
outline of a cloud behind black branches and I wanted to
tell you, day, or weather (surely you're the same thing),

how your rain of events, this endless rain keeps the door
stuck, the hours leaking into air. The rain is what
I am. But how are you, day, and what season are you
bringing in searing bird calls, or a wind that unwraps

the invisible instant, its far-off dust drifting into the edges
of our speech? The isobars move in. On the underside of
atmospheric pressure, time spills in a cloud of what might
never happen, if only it hadn't already. Good. Morning.

THE CELESTIAL SET-UP

imagine staring up into an open umbrella
         you're holding as it pivots

after the defeat after the ruin
         and the flawed reconstruction
    what's left but drawing the body into
its own circle spinning around an axis

not like a small country flailing spikes
      from its malignant crown but in star clusters
islands breaking into archipelagos

by this I mean a network of events
        or love moving on the epidermis
a crackle on a hand
     in the small distance unravelling in tenses
between your past and my future

        performing a horizontal music
in relation to the touch of breath
    or the edge of this poem falling into space
where every revolution is still happening in your skin

when does holding out your hand
        become a question
which way to the centre
      and how will I know when I get there
when the city is both a practice of scars and
     a pattern of what's in the air
        in other words in song
an accumulation of detail invisible until you're dead

for now we wander slowly about the star sphere
        in a discontinuity that exists as aperture
to defer the sound of an ending not to
        stop there just look
                don't look at the sun

this is not the grave of rosa luxemburg she is not here you
will not find her neither will you find her at the memorial
to rosa luxemburg at the lichtenstein bridge or the u-bahn
station rosa-luxemburg-platz you can search the length of
rosa-luxemburg-straße in erfurt you will not find her she
isn't walking down rosa-luxemburg-straße in leipzig or rosa-
luxemburg-straße in chemnitz we need her but she is not here
you can't stop looking on rosa-luxemburg-straße in döbeln but
she isn't there she's not on calle rosa luxemburgo in gijón she's
not at the centre rosa luxemburg in béthune she isn't there
and you won't find her on ulica roze luksemburg in belgrade
you can visit the rosa-luxemburg-stiftung in munich frankfurt
hamburg bremen stuttgart saarbrücken leipzig amsterdam
brussels and méxico but you won't find her you can walk
through the centro commercial rosa luxemburgo in madrid
but she isn't there and neither is she anywhere on calle rosa
luxemburgo or in the colegio público rosa luxemburgo or the
clínica veterinaria rosa luxemburgo all of which are also in
madrid where you won't find her you will not find her on calle
rosa luxemburgo in arganda del rey it wasn't rosa luxemburg
who lit up the róża luksemburg electric lamp factory in warsaw
she is not in the jardins rosa luxemburg in paris or the jardins
de rosa luxemburg in barcelona where although you may find
roses you will not find her it's no use looking for mies van de
rohe's monument to rosa luxemburg and karl liebknecht in
berlin as it's no longer there but if it were you wouldn't find
her and she's not in rosa-luxemburg-platz in dresden or the
collège rosa luxemburg in aubervilliers knock on every door
in ulitsa rozy lyuksemburg in yecaterinburg she isn't there you
will not find her she isn't on lôn rosa lwcsembwrg in llandegfan
nor in the lycée rosa luxemburg in canet-en-roussillon you can

spend days on ulica roza luksemburg in skopje but you won't see her she is not on ulitsa roza luksemburg in sliven you will not find her on calle rosa de luxemburgo in la camocha you will not find her you will not find her there

A MARITIME VOCABULARY

what travessia/trip/travesía/trajet

                          traverses

        the wreck/naufrágio/
naufragio/naufrage

of language underwater

        glimpsed through bones and rafters

whose is this zone/zona/zona/zone

        where I am passenger and cargo

and the anchor is a

        weight/peso/peso/poids

                and nothing floats freely

not even the cargo of words

        while the names of the dead

                are still sinking

this self/mesmo/mismo/soi

        all at sea/mar/mar/mer
no more than a murmur

in the hold/porão/bodega/cale

there may be dates dental instruments

        detergent

                drafting paper dyestuff

or solvents spark plugs spectacles
                staplers sunflower seeds

that is to say
        it's a mixed vessel/navio mixto/
navío mixto/navire mixte
                carrying too much weight

say vessel that is my speech
say mouth
        boca/width/anchura/largeur
                say open sea

STELLAR BEARING PRO FORMA

I am south of lyre
I am north of scorpion
I am east of eagle
I am some way west of swan

          this is my angle of tilt
               how's yours

balancear de una borda a otra   to roll
      to a tipping point

          reach to the brightest star
isolated and little-seen
          noting the altered positions

still   visible

trazar un rumbo   to trace a route
          here we go rumbling on

what lies
          in the water
a sea shaken to its depths

          run your finger
up the left-hand edge

          identify as/with
            constellations
in the second you speak
          a second enters

in the pull and reach
of daily rotation

suppose that

                    lies roughly in line with

    a hand searches air

        light falls
                        behind a minute

a rusting winch
        a chain dragged over rocks

NEWBOROUGH WARREN WITH MAP OF HAVANA

mira y no les descuides.
las islas son mundos aparentes.

> *look and don't neglect them.*
> *the islands are apparent worlds.*
> — Reina María Rodríguez

now you see it
    now
        not that island but another
where birds call
        back to themselves
a stonechat grating rocks
    a sedge warbler riffing on the songs
it stole from everywhere

I'm trying to make this up
    out of the real
how can we live when we're all at sea

the music inside shatters
    on exposure to the air
        invisible bodies in the streets
    move through me
        in a footstep a gesture
a balcony collapses
    the lights blink out

feet slide on sand and small roots
    off the edge of a map where land is
churned to wave form under wind

a marsh harrier turns
      overhead the far-off drone of planes
the warmth is wrong it should be raining
      in another language *lluvia*
                  the sudden downpour
                  between synapses

where *revolución* is letters reflected in a window
whose struggle is that
      whose logo

and it's this way to the Malecón
            to look out over the Menai Strait
where the sea
      pulls every island to itself
a blue expanse holds the sky flat

an apparition of ponies
      shimmers into something you'd believe in
their furious hunger
      teeth locked on tufts of dune grass
while underground the rabbits
          hollow out the dark

and that's my shadow
      where a compass needle falls

THE ISLAND

is land   is the sum total of possible arrangements

is moving north   as constellations travel south   is

freely moving and therefore unpredictable   is no more

than accumulated dust   is an infinite line un-

ravelling against the sea   looks like repetition but is

a means of branching off   is said to be lapsing into a

state of chaos   is neither metaphor nor translation   is

only translation   is neither melting star   nor exploding

ice cube   needs our love   as in collective work   arises

from a state of molecular uncertainty   is less failure of hope

than a problem of distribution   is not a bleeding body

or a blank in a sea chart   is a ring of lights   is the reason

why nothing is ever that simple   goes forward   swirling

mottled   is sidling over whose horizon   is selective

information and kinetic energy   is wave function and

angular momentum   is dispersal   is reordering   is a

slow process   is where we are   is what breaks and breaks

We're waiting for the tide to turn. Every minute there are readings of water, piped in and piped out, algae showing as a ray of light that bounces back on green. Under morning sun, the surface stirs and flicks: this is how it appears, as retreating blue that looks back. But what do I know? Soundings off the sea floor come up in layered patterns as the data stream flows in different intensities: a cobalt speckled band of fish; refracted harmonics of the lower levels. You'd be swayed by the glimpse of a seal led by fish led by movement led by transfer of energy, but who's to say who sways what in the dip and shudder of knowledge, a vessel.

> Relative velocity
> > Real velocity
> Temperature
> > Salinity
> Transmittance
> > Oxygen
> Turbidity
> > Fluorescence

Underwater, you could be anywhere, but here the coast arranges itself at eye level so that what's behind it seems to be solid: mainland on the right and island on the left. Deep in the wreck, the blue glass jar holds nothing but green, nothing but darkness where the cargo, where the money was. There's no-one steering our country. Which country would that be? For the fish, everything joins up. You'd think the sea was an open space but here it's tunnel vision. It took so few to sink us. The raster chart maps the shifting line of a boat through rocks and wrecks, where land is a broken shell around the sea.

Trwyn Du
    Albanian and Nydia
Cambank and Derbent
    East Mouse Middle Mouse West Mouse
The Skerries and East Platters
    Castilian
Tower of Refuge
    Bolivar Rock

Today's catch is data, plural like fish but inedible. An instrument on the sea floor is waiting for acoustic release. Talk to it: no answer. A grapple and both winches, a boss hook on each winch. We scan the horizon for a yellow buoy, but can only see cormorants. It might be underneath the boat or it might come up suddenly, battering the hull. The boat's too near, or too far away. Someone thinks they've seen it: we'll be back before nightfall. Then it's disappeared. The wire unravels into the sea, wavering as it goes. It slackens as it hits the bottom and then it's dragged along. The grappling hook is lowered off the end of the boat, a question in the form of a claw. We really don't know what's down there, says the skipper.

few words a choreography
    down there on the deck
in muscle memory
    they swing around the rope or
all four line up eight
    hands four helmets eight
feet up and down the stairs
    radio messaging

It's pulling something. Yeah, an old boot. The wire snaps taut. Look at that – probably the phone line to the mainland. The grapple comes up empty. Another pass and a cable is looped up, running over pulleys. They cast along it and at last, they've got it, a second cable looped down and attached. *And what is productive labour when it comes to the sea?* The instrument arrives like a miniature space station, hauled up with a train wheel and a tangle of wires. The boat speeds up on course for Menai Bridge. The gadget bleeps forlornly as it's wiped dry, data on its metal discs in rainbow bands of tidal information, unfathomable.

slow dived from noon
        at last shade at least
open water in one vortex
        waves round and round
under oily shimmer
        soundings from space
stars a wilderness flashed
        off the surface

A SHORT PRESENTATION ON THE CURRENT DIRECTION OF TRAVEL

we are where we are we are where we are we are where
we are we are where we are we are where we are we are
where we are we are where we are we are where we are
we are where we are we are where we are we are where
we are we are where we are we are where we are we are
where we are we are where we are we are where we are
we are where we are we are where we are we are where
we are we are where we are we are where we are we are
where we are we are where we are we are where we are
we are where we are we are where we are we are where
we are we are where we are we are where we are we are
where we are we are where we are we are where we are
we are where we are we are where we are we are where
we are we are where we are we are where we are we are

DISPLACEMENT FIXING BY STEERAGE

Prepaid freight

To avoid the postcard of collision at a later platform, three settlements of threat will be explained for the outsider. They are i) the cardinal policing of contraband, ii) bilge, and iii) the different tonnage we employ. If you stand facing notices to mariners (i.e. towards scope, if you are in engine or war risk), space is behind you, ebb is on your right harbour, whirlwind on your left harm. A berth is a horizontal arrest measured clockwise.

The Statement of Account

The procedure for finding one's weight in an unknown current is one of many with which experienced marine reconnaissance can assist. In a setback as you travel southward, the constructive total loss appears to drift northward over your heaviest hatch. If you have a vigilante, you need not worry about marking the earlier quotas. All you have to do is mark the shift in information.

Receipt in Full of All Demands

The police state is not conspicuously bright. Unless the medical advice of the helmsman be clearly understood, the noon SOS remains a bewildering and disordered allocation. Once you know its approximate signal, the cocktail party of the H-hour in which it is to be found, and its varying postscripts, a few mists in the opening of a starlit non-delivery should be sufficient for you to locate and recognise the policy, even if you have never seen or heard of it before.

The Next Storm

The statements contain many approximate infractions of directives which are only to be detected by the knowing facility of the Mare Nostrum who is 'at hook' among the snotters. Once one understands the medium of the daily and annual channels in the approach of the noon sound, and can in addition recognise the brighter spaces, it is quite impossible to be entirely lost on a clear note: one may not be able to say more than 'That is roughly echo', or 'Squall is more or less over there', but this is enough to guard against complete displacement.

The Plumb and the Pool Start

Let us now turn our attention from the supercargo to the non-slip. The berth of the statements will be briefly described later, and at this point it is only necessary to say that whereas the positions of the statements in the slipway are continuously altering, there is *one* statement whose position is steadfast. And this statement is located directly above the N. point of the hour. No matter from what point of ebb's northern hindrance you look at it, it is always within one delivery of true note.

A DIVINATORY CALENDAR

ce xóchitl
1 flower

The rain has stopped, lavender and eucalyptus
crushed between fingers. Blue scatters on the stones,
a fluttering of ash against the skin. It hurts to live in words
but whose hurt is it, so far from the catastrophe unfolding
right in front of you, a continuous downward movement.

ome cipactli
2 crocodile

Times overlap on a day caught in the teeth of calendared
events snapping shut on the possibility of doing all of this again
in someone else's life. I'm trying to speak to this moment but it's
not listening. The habits of highly productive people include lying
down at the crossroads covered in ash. Avoid meetings.

ye ehécatl
3 wind

From the cardinal points held in balance by a mid-air
somersault, everything comes undone in your hands, you
waiting at the centre of the flood ready to crash down
on all the messages marked URGENT jajajajaja,
your inbox the dimensions of the known world.

naui calli
4 house

The explosions are coming closer. Electricity, sound waves
and love, you said, they're all the same thing. I said maybe
translations of each other, as if translation were a metaphor
but you said no, they are identical. On the other side of the wall
it's getting dark. I shut my eyes against the flickering lights.

macuilli cuetzpalin
5 lizard

Old days scuttle through the new or stop and freeze. Don't
look at your watch or the clocks painted on plates,
only if you must the one in the square that has no hands.
And if I stole this day you're just as much
a thief hiding in the crack between calendars.

chiquace cóatl
6 snake

Coiled loops of sun make each hour a repeatable circle
spiralling down as you follow the lines of force to see where
they break. Pointless having a to-do list. There are 1440 minutes
in a day, some of which you remember and others that fall
into this system of dismembering known as work or conquest.

chicome miquiztli
7 death

In the cross-fade of two musics, memory and waiting
become a single tension in the sound of your heart still
beating through the hours to keep the sun beaming down
in dollars, pesos, pounds, the natural order. Get to the point
just when it dissolves like salt in drizzle bristling the skin.

chicuei mázatl
8 deer

A deer runs from the trees, its ears curved out to motorways
and stars. Infinity catches in the branches. Believe me when I say
that all of this was accidental. Now none of it. It's only
repetitions, diaries and divinations that bring what's outside
inside, folding habit round the smashed glass and roadkill.

chiconaui tochtli
9 rabbit

You may just be a rabbit but look at the sky. Everyone
remembers your image in light. Productive people use the night
before to plan the day ahead, always finding time to sit
at the roadside staring into a field where a man is picking
yellow flowers for the ceremonies before the rain comes.

matlactli atl
10 water

After the rain I'm looking for a colour for this word,
petrichor. Plant oil seeping into earth could be
green, but blood is just as volatile. Take this
blush reddening the air when thunder rolls back
the curtain on a massacre that hasn't ended yet.

matlactli once itzcuintli
11 dog

The dog on the roof howls its own dog song to afternoon,
which growls back distantly with traffic. I can't hear what
you're saying, the shape of your lips drowned out
by the seconds blurred into white noise, while the last
bird in a storm is trying to pronounce its name.

matlactli omome ozomatli
12 monkey

The car slows down just where the volcano frames
the church on the pyramid. Calculate exposure times
in centuries or look away now. I'm all of these split-second
collisions, not to speak of the monkey in the blood jumping
backwards and forwards between them. And running late.

matlactli omei malinalli
13 grass

Water speaks and grains of maize speak, a mass of earth speaks against the histories of stars, a buzzing in the night. Grass busy underfoot. You clap your hands. It's not the birds that answer back, it's time that shrieks. The days are talking all at once, their tongues punctured with green blades.

Cholula, 2016

if anyone asks who you are   say you are nobody   and no
body is washed up   on the shores of this poem   and nobody
can sing when everything   conspires   to   shut   you   up   and
the song doesn't   start anywhere or ever finish   the frame
collapses and this love   won't stay out of that one   flashed up
on a screen too fast   to read the name   filmed with voice-
overs or washed away   sailing the wine-blue   to peoples of
alien speech   your words are like the words of what changes
in the blood   eating the flowers made me forget the way
home   in a structure that was just an accretion this was   the
music   my mind moved along the info stream assimilating
which is not to say becoming similar   the thread of a life takes
form   in an eye travelling down   for surely your words are
like an octopus   dragged with pebbles in its suckers   like the
wash of the great sea   like an island on the edge of an island
like seafall sucked over stones   in the grip of the sea   I forgot
my own name   an assemblage of cells   here the eyes   there
the oiled skin   and grey-eyed Athene went away with the
likeness of a vulture   for the dead are very close   to the edge
of the world   translucent fish and islands in luminous water
in the wake of the ship interrupting itself   where a passport
is a hollow vessel   this face is like your face   you pass with
biometric data   where all the eyes had turned into a single
eye   and the shutters go down   you arrive in the likeness
of a gannet   and the shutters shut against you   and who put
out the giant eye   it was nobody my name is nobody   in the
likeness of an owl   to allow the bearer to pass freely   without
let or hindrance   in the name of every which way wind   as
when an octopus is dragged from its shelter   so the rocks
tore at his skin   so the storm that was in my heart   raged
as weather systems whorled like fingerprints   what word

escapes your teeth's barrier   when you speak of them coming
out of the sea   encrusted with salt   what it means to be
leaving in the likeness of a cormorant   so many leaving in
the likeness of a seagull   so many leaving in the likeness of a
heron   so many leaving in the likeness of an egret   so who
are you   do you remember our bed made of a still-rooted olive
do you remember our bed planed with a brazen adze   a place
without right of seizure   skin bathed clean of salt and rubbed
with oil   such assistance and protection as necessary   the
singer was blind and he was nobody   they were struggling
up the sides of the ship   with ropes and ladders   their hands
and feet were cut and slipping   these feet are like your feet
my heart was a storm in me as I went   and the journeying
ways were darkened   this face is like your face and these
hands are like your hands

ANECDOTE FOR THE BIRDS

From a line by Geeshie Wiley

The last kind words I heared my daddy say

were not the ones about the wallpaper that he
misquoted like everyone else, and which were not
in any case the last words of Oscar Wilde. He looked
at the owl on a chain around my neck and said

it was an owl for wisdom, but I can't remember
the sound of the words, only how I understood them
as a wish, or a carving of feathers, meaning I didn't
hear them at all. Now there's only something muffled,

a bad line. When you asked about poetry and birdsong,
I misheard *parrot* as *parent*, guessing you meant
the give and take of words in love or imitation
that might be the same thing, my singing to you

across the sea in sounds from someone else's
throat. Oh I *heared*, yes I *heared* you. Look, there's
a buzzard. And there's a starling mimicking its cat-call.
Against the background hiss of sky it's my voice

deepening with others that won't let themselves
be buried. Just leave me out. All the same notes
and suddenly it's a different song, the birds with
open beaks and a music that would eat me whole.

RED SQUIRRELS IN COED CYRNOL

1.

Let's say the sky's all yours
       in a jump for thin branches
shy crowns giving flight
       to impossible belief
           its luminescence
      falling through canopy
when you're all claws
      in stellar twigs bud clusters
            streaked inside with sap
        a hidden line unfolding
while shadows hold still
      on shattered glass

Whose spiral and spring
        comes on the hour
    on time we say
         but whose

2.

The grip of morning
   never lets you down
carries you into
    highwires of pines
      their vertical tang

Between entering the forest
     and saying
everything at once
   is an improvised green
     the soft response of moss
while the understory tangles
   holly for ash
sycamore for elder
     drawing down light to our
pedestrian skulls
    blunt fingers
   grounded and peripheral

3.

Today the sea's sucked out
        below the island's lunar edges
here we are lugging our minerals
           through the woods
arranging the world in the eye
       I speak to it I speak to you
          and you
leap between
          trees that are not islands

           Look
at these edges open to trap
      the air that holds you
          buoyed up by song
        and it's true that hair is *everything*
           your red brush
                 stroke
shivers poised

      What poison and death
           in my idea of wild

4.

I can't write down
              these flights
where tensed paw
       electric fur
             where pointed ear
    errs
where gap
        in air

     now paused on never

A smudge against bark
       becomes an outline
             of tail flick and bitten twig
a scuttle into ivy
       tentative nesting
          a repetition
of scribbled movement
            paths written over

5.

Today I stare up for signs
        of life that doesn't
                flash itself around
        when the world has scarpered
here behind the stage
        searching for a lightning zig
zag
        hot glamour

I'm dizzy from looking up at this
        dimension in which I can't exist
where I'm no longer sure that you do
        where holding a space is bloodshed
                as the day crushes in
where if we're anything
                  we're in it here
        if not together

Why should you give yourself up
in a code I can read
        here at the kerb and waiting
eyes left
            no
                    right then left
            or was it right
        a forest scatters into traffic

6.

It's movement that pulls us
through
            in step
       too far behind to catch
a blur that won't take shape
              in the eye
 and its demands
             I don't know what I want
except
       to follow tree to tree
the length of a broken continent
      never once
           touching the ground
where shells lie cracked
           in dead leaves
I can't feel your
      sprung muscle
           dimensions of light
the tap of claws on bark
            gingering up
the weightless routine
       let's call it life
here's your hunger
      mine too

7.

Where were you now
            in this blank dazzle
in forked routes and fizz of wings
        splintered in pins and needles
embroidered
        with another sun
                    the flourish
of an inked silhouette
                    bursting into
tree-form
        star-form unravelling
and running on
                through the twists
and breaks
        in the phrase that never comes
                        to a halt
        in the junction
                    of branches and breath

VOYAGE

close by is a silver branch
etched with frost I couldn't
tell you where the twigs end
and the white flowers begin

bearing a kind of glitter
baring the edge of blue
pebbles churn underwater
mutating colours of the sea

in yesterday's weather cloud
glistens in ridges of sand
turning on a mussel shell
there in the mist behind the sky

dolphins and porpoises leap
in rings around the island birds
call to the hours there is music
somewhere playing silently

a storm is passing through
eyes far off in the distance
I can't turn into a picture
with receding perspective

there were two blackbirds on the
branch and a single robin now
the robin is gone and a
single blackbird is waiting

CALLER ID

Call it the edges of your breath or a crack where
the wind comes in. Call it the shape of the room,

call it a trap. Call it the cry of a gull giving you
side eye from next door's roof; call it a holding

pattern, a weighing up of currents. Call it song
flattened in the network where I equals another I,

unequal. Call it the page, which is not what I am
saying, here – to you – hanging on a wave, where

sudden red comes bursting into eyeshot. Call it
blossom's slow explosion in the window: don't

listen to it. This glass and wood, call it hallucination.
When sleep is what you clutch at, this is the voice

that calls between your fingers. Call it the taste
of a broken island, call it sand, call it sifting dust.

Call it the catch of sun in the corner. Call this
screen a self, the click and hold, a data trail

of trees in storm light. Call it the distance
of a skin from things around it crowding in,

calling from rock, from falling meteorite.
Call it wrong number (again) and call it back.

NEW MEMORY

well if you're talking about
metaphor
blah blah blah
OK so the idea being
I don't want
yeah and
I'm just going to go
back and look at that
ah no I think we're frozen
yes so I have it I have it
yeah ah oh I've lost you
I can't hear properly
yeah it's me
this is probably the
I think this is
let's give it a minute
it says I have a new memory
yeah this
right that's better that's better
you're back I always think
it's crucial the expression
one got frozen into
you know
so I was thinking about what
falls what falls from the mouth
I mean in the sense of gravity
or accident or just
what's holding
what's holding it all up

IS TEMPORARILY UNABLE

oops something went wrong
                    a gash of light
            letting in a wound
or stump of something
            barely explained
            and oozing too close

a rustle of feathers
                    typographic
insects
            caught in the beak
descenders flailing towards
interpretation
            or fatal error

improbable plant
            a chancy green
                    flickers on
while underneath
            the worms
don't currently have access
            soft bodies brushed back
on the dark side of the slabs

MIGRATION

If that's the 1980s unspooling
from a dusty cassette
(time is what rattles),

this legacy of cloud is where
you're caught in wind, rain,
a superposition of waves:

yes, there is magnetism,
but the magnet you carry
is a glued-on name

unstuck at the edges of
a song still echoing in code
after code, a knot of scenes

in which you're dropping
things, a ring in a crater
or a laptop in a glassy pool,

all of them falling away
from this foothold
on a tuft of bog grass.

THE BED

Our bed was never made from a still-rooted olive
our bed was never planed with a brazen adze
our bed was from Manchester and had extra adjustable storage units
our bed was made of leaves and grasses gathered before the storm
our bed was adrift in an empty cinema where the film had stopped
our bed was several inches too short for us and so was the duvet
our bed was a Chinese lilo in a leaking tent
our bed was digging creases nightly in our foreheads
our bed was swallowing a year for every hour we slept in it
our bed was a cut-price mattress from Finneys' closing-down sale
our bed was two singles stuck together
our bed was the gap in the middle we fell into
our bed was a bed of nails glittering in the dark
our bed was a crevasse where the snow was still falling
our bed was lit by slowly turning planets
our bed was an underpass echoing with traffic
our bed was northbound on the southbound M6
our bed was too small for our cramped arms
our bed was a home for tiny invisible creatures
our bed was balanced on an outcrop of radioactive rock
our bed was a ramshackle space station mended with a butter knife
our bed was where a passing leopard made a sound like moving furniture
our bed was never the same bed as yesterday's
our bed was an accidental collision of feathers and wood
our bed repeated itself endlessly
our bed was a process of disintegration
our bed was a white field and a lost contact lens
our bed was in someone else's room and we didn't notice

ONE STOP

Because I'd forgotten something, possibly what I was
doing there in the first place or where I'd come from,
I meant to go back one stop on the train where
behind me the Tatra mountains rose up improbably
on the border of two wrong countries and then I was
going to return to where you were waiting, but
the train was a high-speed TGV, though it wasn't in
France, and it kept going for three hours, and when
I arrived I couldn't pronounce the name of the place,
which was made of three consonants, maybe K, Z
and Y or was it X, T and S and a number three,
so I couldn't let you know where I was and couldn't
phone you anyway because my phone charger
was in the suitcase I'd left on the platform with you
so I tried my old mobile, which was still in my pocket,
although the keys were all worn out and I couldn't
remember the code, which might have been two
one one four or was it one three seven eight or
nine three eight one or seven two six four or two
five four one or eight eight four three or nine seven
three two or six two one three or one two three four.

FROM TORTUGUERO

You'd have loved this anhinga
spreading out its wings to dry
after rain, the posing heron,
toucans in the tops of trees
I try to photograph for you –

but you're gone like the bodies
slithering languidly into mud
where the hanging shadows
in dripping tangles of lianas
melt suddenly into leaves.

It was something and nothing, life
thickening in warmth and water,
all its abundance moving away,
running deeper into the forest
of if-then-else, now this.

TELESCOPE

In the shadows, a lit score reveals itself
as a moving diagram, a miniature stage

for perforated music flooding through
the gaps. What falls in the missed

beat is an unfolding of the senses to a
memory that hasn't yet arrived. Eyes

in the back of your head blink hexagonal
on insect progress, likelihood of storm.

It's all behind you now, tomorrow going up
in flames on some planet or another where

the pull of what's out of reach has a name
thought to be untranslatable, as if it were

an arrow to a fixed point in seething mineral
aggregates, not a branching into constellations.

The vibration of trees is a coolness or
extended note the length of a human gut

that's wound around its others, a longing
for what's invisible: this radio shimmer.

What eye's not shaped by its technologies?
The extension of skin into galvanised steel,

fatigue-cracks and lunar lens is the wound
of listening with a whole body, concave

and reflective. The relation turns outwards,
its frequency a stop-start jump to somewhere

else, while swelling and contracting stars
pulsate like bells. See what sounds. I can

hear you not humming along, your head
tilting round on its tracks, the sky ringing.

Jodrell Bank, 2022

ADAR MÔN *BIRDS OF ANGLESEY*

GYLFINIR CURLEW *NUMENIUS ARQUATA*

fluting shade
                fluting on water
                                it's spring sun
it's war again (still) and it's
                scissor and scalpel
                                into the sludge
a curlew calling
                on the edge of Europe
                                errant in whose airspace
skydarkling croon
                confused alarms tactic
                                tactic and strategy
here come invisible hounds
                the dead vibrating out of voice
                                in instant composition
or composition of instants
                a courier running
                                and losing ground in lieu
in lieu of this
                tidal absence
                                just about holding a tune

Mulfran Cormorant *Phalacrocorax carbo*

in the middle of a conversation
                    goes incognito
                                        slipping off its names
fifty-three seconds
                    forty-eight seconds
                                        twenty-seven seconds
where do you go
                    when you're not here
                                        leaving the surface
of a morning beside itself
                    in whose future
                                        you dive beneath
advancing positions
                    how do you measure
                                        the distance from water
to water to what
                    can't be scored
                                        in subaqueous punctuation
your shattered bleat
                    on the wind
                                        impossible speech

Pioden Fôr Oystercatcher *Haematopus Ostralegus*

lined up on the shore
            snipping brightly at oh whatever
                        there's too much to read
in the mud these letters
            that float at the centre
                      of things we're
on the side of
            cracked open
                    where I'm alive
I'm a stranger
            squeaking in drizzle
                    orange-pink legs
beak against monochrome
            cockle drill hammer and
                    tongs going each of us
several already
            and stranger still
                    flexed wingspan
this muscle of belonging
            on the no-joke horizon
                    how far will it extend

Pioden Magpie *Pica Pica*

here's one for sorrow
    I salute you when
        twice sadness equals joy
in the mathematics
    of encounter
        as I become your double
in disappearance
    into hawthorn
        in bramble and gorse
in a wink
    hey good morning
        and how are your kin
my kith in this
    flickering day
        where we both know
any win against the sun
    is chequered at best
        and where it falls
you flash your black
    wing on white
        black squared

Mwyalchen Blackbird *Turdus Merula*

presence oozes out of
        habitat all over the place
                a history
in overtones and feedback
        the next phrase
                to be decided
it's all over
        before the beginning
                as distance collapses
into feathered sky
        where this is what I'd say
                to you in an outline
of predictable movement
        clockwise around the morning
                in overlapping rings
around your eyes
        I'm on the path
                you didn't make
or you're in mine
        a thinking body
                quick quick

Telor yr Helyg Willow Warbler *Phylloscopus trochilus*

>>>//::: fitis //>>::

>>/>>piecuszek >>//>>

>>///>>:: fitiszfüzike ::// >>>

>>///>> pouillot fitis >>::///>>

>>///:::: luí grosso ///>>:://

//>>:: mosquitero musical ::// >>>

/::// :::>> felosa-musical :::// >>>

>>>//:: kuchamsitu >>///>::

///>>:::>>kucha-mbuga >>//::

//::/>>>::: timba >>//::

//::/>>>//:: niini ::// >>

///::::// pilipili-sa-mabelete >>>//

//::// >>>hofsanger ::// >>

>>>>///unothoyi ::>>//

DID IT BEGIN
                    with the nest
          or the egg
a gathering of twigs
          or yodelling into wind
a circle of silence
          unspoken yellow
or a listening that speckles
the surface
          breast heat
          under feathers

I stare at my screen
you sit on your clutch

HOW MUCH OF THIS
is sticking to the spot
attention as warm blood
pulsing over shell
          still here
          but millefeuille
not a proper nest
not property but air
          moving through
a single feather
          hollow keratin

BETWEEN TILTED EYE
        and the feathered
        gap that is an ear
lowered head
        beak thrown back
calling into grey
                what is it
                what stays
after image
        in unstable frequencies
        flitting off the roof
                and winging it again

YOUR REFLECTION MUDDLES
        the jellyfish bloom
sleek head
        shattered
        in ripple form
                an insatiable thirst
for the chewed-up sea
        in play
nownownow
                in the present
performance of morning

CIRCLE AND LAND
    the sweep up
        the angle
   to the ground
       where rhythm
is a moving shape
    wing scrawl
       unfinished
swagger and roll
    on pink feet
is gull is gull is
    gull chick waltz
       to the beak's red spot

EVERY BIRD
    has the outline of another
over the horizon
    sea cloudcloudcloud edge
of sunset
       skull sculpted
in streaks of winter plumage

       arrowing
in brittle air
    a cry
that doesn't reach
    to where the sky comes down

HOW FAR CAN YOU SEE
from the same place
        daily wheeling
around the town

        lamp post telegraph pole
        pebble dot sky massed cloud
        bird shadow double

                        so what
do you think
        when thinking is watching
is waiting is sudden flurry
is intensified air is flight
        is a disappearing line

CELESTE STOP

For Jeff Hilson

pipes tuned off pitch
          speak together in an undulation
or shimmer imitating strings
another hic another nunc

the hautboy is a swelling
hautboy placed in its own swell box

the case has swell shutters in the roof
and both are operated by the same swell pedal

it is like watching hands moving and not
seeing them
                    or dancing it is like dancing
with invisible feet on the pedals

or a writer writing air in its own swell box
          mood music swelling down the aisles
interfering with the mechanism
                    and the voicing
a shadow memory ahead of every note

a hautboy is not an oboe and a stopped
diapason is not a diapason but a flute

hands and feet and pumping arm
in an England without organs
                    reversed into tomorrow

while in St Burchardi Church in Halberstadt
the note has changed
                    and time moves as slowly
as possible in both directions
                    on and on until 2640
oh future here we come

pull out all the stops for stars
and their variations
                    bright in the talking air
nunc dimittis on the console hey let's go

CRÉTEIL

After Les Choux de Créteil by Gérard Grandval

it's the end of the
blossom by the
zoom into 1960s
on the outer ring

lilac line and bushes
cabbage buildings
space clusters
each sculpted leaf

hanging with potential ungrown
gardens barely pushing above
the concrete absent cascades
of green down temple curves

where lives repeat
haven't taken off but
with hope buried in
provisional grass

in rockets that
stayed growing
the cabbage fields
roots waiting

at the point where the city ex-
plodes on contact with the sky
its force field propels us into
slow traffic the sun radiating

these days laced
a car's metal roof
where everything
of the senses

together under
a sound box pulsing
pushes out to the edge
in a slow eruption

balanced on concrete stems
every balcony's a sleeping ear
turned up to the sky's blank
transmission of tomorrow

in rounded walls
adjust to curvature
that doesn't stack up
out of reach but still

where fittings don't
mould to life
in the circumference
traced by your fingers

DURING THE WORKS

After Apollinaire

There was a whine of
builders' drills and cables hung
in loops beyond the half-done
shopfronts of the Forum des Halles
underground cloisters
on old cemetery limits

Mannequins grimaced
vacant in spring neons
and it set my teeth on edge
this razzle of fashion eternally
consuming its own death

Suddenly
rapid as memory
their eyes lit up
from glazed cell to glazed cell

Mythologies shattered in the glass
and the dummies accosted me
with their otherworld faces
in the fourth circle of FNAC
Apollinaire's *Alcools* in my hand

If their arm bones and leg
bones had long since gone to be
stacked in the catacombs
the leftovers unsettled
by the works had been
translated into fibreglass

And now they'd woken up
all at once less funereal
even laughing
at their own reflections

Had this been life? So much
glitter and striplight so much
money and love yes call it that

At that moment I loved them too

They looked at me tenderly
looked through me at
Apple Nikon Hitachi Samsung
galaxies unfolding in their stares

I said why don't we go for a walk

The shadows and their shadows
went voguing up the escalator
gliding arm in arm past Zara past
L'Occitane a whiff of lavender
or rosemary

We rose towards the surface and
blinked into sun

All forty-nine of them
lurched into the newly-planted
meadow crushing cowslips dancing
to the busker's violin that scratched
No woman no cry

A startled tourist stopped
photographing magnolias
as the dead mingled with the living

A stiff hand unclenched
a student took it
you're the one he said
I'll wait ten years for you
or twenty

I'll wait all your life for you she said

Behind them the tune
switched to *Will the circle*
be unbroken

Another of the dead was trying to charm
a girl in a yellow shift
accessorized in black
a feather clipped in her hair
I love you he said
as New Look loves Dior
or sunglasses love the eyes of stars

Too late the girl replied her hands
shaking her wedding ring glinting

Construction workers in their
yellow hats went by
fluorescent jackets flicking back sun
from the site of the Holy Innocents

We threw small change into
the fountain and watched it sink

There was a smell of scorched
metal from the building site
where they were rigging a wave
of saffron glass above the shops

Our most extravagant desires
were echoed back at us
and the couples went on talking
with their lovely mouths

We could be so happy here
said the dead man to the living girl
see how the waves would close
over our heads you wouldn't know
if it was yourself you saw in the
glass or me looking back at you
there would only be longing
disembodied as markets
pure as angels or diamonds

But I can see that you're afraid
and perhaps rightly so
there would be no turning back

At last we found ourselves
returning to the temporary
entrance and its sign

Pendant les travaux
le shopping continue

The living started drifting off
saying bye for now
see you later and going
for a coffee in Costa or browsing
Esprit or H&M while their
remaining hours and minutes
ticked away in Swatch

The dead went back to the windows
and took up their poses with no
idea of what had happened
I spotted one of them in Gap
and another in Etam
but they didn't
catch my eye

There's nothing so uplifting
as having loved the dead
you lose yourself in glassy
reflection you're strong for life
and you don't need anyone

HELLO MOON

After Laforgue

Hello, wrinkled toads who guard the mountains,
snapping your teeth at the baby turtle doves
who can't stop grooving to your tunes!

Hello, glow-in-the-dark whales! And you
outmoded swans as beautiful as battleships,
observe this whole catastrophe drifting by!

And you, white peacocks flashing disco glitter,
and you foetuses, your bald domes so contemporary,
sphinxes browsing ennui with brass moustaches,
who, by the scrolling waters of the basalt caves,
ruminate to eternity! Immortal chewing gum!

Yes, reindeer with crystal antlers! Polar bears
as sad as three wise men, strolling with folded arms
to honeys of beatific silence! Porcupines
pointlessly aiming your vicious pens!

Yes, butterflies of jewelled ink, open your
wings to the flickering pages of this screen!

Yes, pale jelly hippopotami, floating
masses that light up nervous systems,
intestinal pythons writhing in brains of dead
abstraction! Elephants crumble in a breath!

And you, frozen flowers! Mandrake faces,
cacti obelisks with your fruit in tombs,
massive candle forests, gardens of polyps,
white coral palms with steel resins!

Marble lilies with hysterical smiles, play
your dawn music for a hundred years
then spill the milk that will be yours!
Mushrooms, spring up like palaces!

we'd hoped to see the
aurora borealis
as if another
sky could open on the same
horizon but we're
staring at the edge of an
island drawing in

what's walking in me
what's talking in the swell of
a marginal sea
of the Atlantic Ocean
the unseen outline
of what hasn't yet arrived
where codes in me break
into unsingable sound
unsoundable song

hard to see which way is north
or up given that
a bear looks so little like
a bear a lion
so unlike a lion this
is where we are now
on a small burning planet
where vegetables are
marked with flags and days inch by
in columns what fills
the spaces what patterns what
margins of error

underneath the head's own hum
faces turn to wind
where summer chatters on the
wires what key does your
ear sing in tell me how to
rearrange the chords
in the brain sing it once more
in sediments now
we're listening to the foldback

suddenly lucid
and awake still a statue
filling up space a
memorial to the wrong
battle everyone
wants to forget but whose dream
do you remember
if you can't smell it are you
sure that it exists
in black and white film where steam
from coffee must be
translated by subtitles
the scent of music
now chip off the letters as
the lone and level
microplastics drift from view

'Weather this' was commissioned by Julia Fiedorczuk for *Przekrój*, Poland.

'A Rose for Rosa' was written for *The Graveside Orations of Carl Einstein*, edited by Dale Holmes and Sharon Kivland (Ma Bibliothèque, 2019).

The italicised line is from Fredric Jameson in the *London Review of Books* (Vol. 42 No 8, 2020). 'A Maritime Vocabulary', 'Stellar Bearing Pro Forma' and https://www.lrb.co.uk/the-paper/v42/n08. 'Displacement Fixing by Steerage' make use of J.B. Sidgwick's *Direction Finding by the Stars* (Faber and Faber, 1944) and Sydnea Meyer Philbert's *Vocabulário Marítimo Internacional* (1975).

'Newborough Warren with a Map of Havana' was written during the process of making *Here be Dragons* with Paul Farley and Geoff Bird (BBC Radio 4, 7 April, 2019).

'A Strait Story' draws on a trip on Research Vessel Prince Madog in June 2017, for which I am grateful to the crew and especially Ben Powell.

'If anyone asks' was written as part of a collaboration with Nia Davies called 'Mare Nostrum', first performed as part of the Gelynion: Wales – Enemies tour, which Nia co-organised with Steven Fowler in May 2015. A version of this work was made into a video by Daniel Leeman & Jessica Raby for the *New Welsh Review*. https://vimeo.com/154887400. My thanks to Nia both for the collaboration and her permission for the re-use of my contribution to it.

'Anecdote for the Birds' was written at the invitation of Peter Riley for *Last Kind Words* (Shearsman, 2021), an anthology of poems responding to a song by Geeshie Wiley.

Part of 'Voyage' was published in *Triongl* (Cyhoeddiadau'r Stamp, 2021), edited by Iestyn Tyne, in response to photography by Lena Jeanne.

'Telescope' refers to Tom Raworth's comment: 'I really have no sense of questing for knowledge. At all. My idea is to go the other way, you know. And to be completely empty and then see what sounds.' 'Tom Raworth – An Interview', interview by Barry Alpert, 11 February 1972, *Vort* 1 (Fall 1972), p. 39.

'Adar Môn *Birds of Anglesey*' takes its title from the book of that name by Peter Hope Jones and Paul Whalley (Menter Môn, 2004), and some sections were published in *Migrating Knowledges: Science, Subjectivity and Landscape*, edited by Joey Frances and Jo Wright (2022), as part of a project funded by the Natural Environment Research Council responding to the nature notebooks of Dr Paul Whalley in Bangor University Archives.

'Gullscape' takes its title from a painting by Roy Lichtenstein, 1964.

'Celeste Stop' was published in *Hilson Hilson*, edited by Richard Parker (The Crater Press, 2020). It refers to Jeff Hilson's poems and to his comment: 'And is the church organ itself not a hauntological instrument, simultaneously both backward and forward looking? Old-fashioned in its outmoded religious contexts, it is futuristic in its use of the console, a name given to the organ's keyboard, stops and pedals as well as of course to the operating systems of any number of real and fictional spacecraft.' Jeff Hilson, 'The God-Awful Small Affair of the Invisible Organist: David Bowie Translated', *English: Journal of the English Association*, Volume 69, Issue 267, Winter 2020, p. 351.

'During the Works' translates Guillaume Apollinaire's 'La maison des morts', and was written during a residency at Les Récollets, Paris in 2014.

'Hello Moon' is a partial translation of Jules Laforgue's 'Climat, faune et flore de la lune,' commissioned by Susannah V. Evans.

Some of the poems were first published in *The Celestial Set-Up* (Oystercatcher, 2020); *Blackbox Manifold*; *B O D Y*, and the *Golden Handcuffs Review*. Many thanks to all the editors. My thanks, too, to Michael Schmidt, John McAuliffe and Andrew Latimer at Carcanet.

I am grateful for a fellowship from the Arts and Humanities Research Council that enabled me to work on this collection.